Jim Thorpe

SUPERSTAR LINEUP

JIM THORPE
20TH-CENTURY JOCK

ROBERT LIPSYTE

HarperTrophy
A Division of HarperCollinsPublishers

...ments

...copyright holders of all copyrighted
materials and secure the necessary permission to reproduce them. In the event of
any questions arising as to their use, the publisher will be glad to make changes
in future printings and editions.

In addition, the publisher acknowledges the following institutions and
individuals for the illustrations provided to us: Page viii: Courtesy of Southwest
Museum, Los Angeles, California; page 8: The Warner Collection of Gulf States
Paper Corp., Tuscaloosa, Alabama; page 12: Woolaroc Museum, Bartlesville,
Oklahoma; page 19: Francis G. Mayer/Photo Researchers; page 26: The
Bettmann Archive; pages 32, 33, 41, 48, 57, 59, 61, 64, 66, 74, 75, 79:
Cumberland County Historical Society, Carlisle, Pennsylvania; pages 40, 63, 81,
84, and 87: Hall of Fame/NFL Photos; page 92: UPI/Bettmann; page 94: Rick
Hill/Lacrosse USA, Inc.

★

Jim Thorpe
20th-Century Jock

Library of Congress Cataloging-in-Publication Data
Lipsyte, Robert.
  Jim Thorpe : 20th-century jock / by Robert Lipsyte.
     p. cm. — (Superstar lineup)
  Summary: A biography of the American Indian known as one of the best all-
round athletes in history for his accomplishments as an Olympic medal winner
and as an outstanding professional football and baseball player.
  ISBN 0-06-022988-8. — ISBN 0-06-022989-6 (lib. bdg.)
  ISBN 0-06-446141-6 (pbk.)
  1. Thorpe, Jim, 1887–1953—Juvenile literature. 2. Athletes—United
States—Biography—Juvenile literature. 3. Indians of North America—
Biography—Juvenile literature. 4. Athletes, Indian—United States—Juvenile
literature. [1. Thorpe, Jim, 1887–1953. 2. Athletes. 3. Indians of North
America—Biography.] I. Title. II. Series.
GV697.52.T5L57   1993   92-44069
796.'092—dc20   CIP
[B]   AC

Typography by Tom Starace

First Harper Trophy edition, 1995

★

This page is for my team.

Robert Warren, my editor, and Theron Raines, my agent, were smart and steady coaches.

Kathy Sulkes, my wife, was the photo researcher who never quit.

Professor Peter Levine of Michigan State University checked the manuscript with his Captain History eye.

Benjamin Kabak, a student at the Horace Mann—Barnard School in New York, was a very helpful reader.

And without the editing, writing and research of Sam Lipsyte, there would be no pages after this one.

★

Jim Thorpe

In 1884, three years before Jim was born, this Yuman Runner of the Southwest was poised to run a marathon at a moment's notice and deliver a message that could save his Nation.

Prologue

The first athletes of America were the Runners of the native Nations, the people who have come to be called Indians. These Runners were fast and dependable and smart. They memorized messages that might take hours to tell, and they remembered them for days at a time, while running through unfamiliar, sometimes hostile territory. Then, after delivering the long message, a Runner might even be expected to help negotiate a peace treaty, work out an alliance for war, offer advice in a sensitive political situation or take another long message back home.

The Runners were heroes, admired for their intelligence, their dedication and their athletic skills, which they kept at peak performance by regular training. It was a full-time job; they ran thousands of miles in preparation for their journeys, studied with their tribal wisdom keepers and ate vegetables, grains and the meat of swift creatures such as antelope and quail.

Sometimes they competed against each other in public races, betting clothes and jewelry. In their daily lives of exercise and careful nutrition and relaxation, of listening to older Runners and to the Chiefs, they were like modern athletes. Yet the importance of their duties made them similar to modern diplomats and journalists. They bound their world together with their savvy and their speed.

They ran the Iroquois Trail in what is now upstate New York. They found ways to ford the swollen spring rivers of the Midwest, and they made their own paths through dense southern forest. They clawed up the sheer rock cliffs of the Pacific Coast.

In 1680, in the cool of the Southwest night, pairs of Pueblo Indian Runners coursed over the high desert in what is now northern New Mexico, carrying messages coded into carved sticks and knotted strings. Their mission was to signal the Pueblo Indians to rise up against the Spanish colonists who had taken control of their villages, burned their sacred masks and flogged their religious leaders. For the Runners, discovery meant instant death. But timidity was worse; if they were late, if the attack wasn't precisely coordinated, the revolt would fail and thousands of Indians would be killed. The Runners were successful, and so was the Pueblo uprising; it was an American revolution a century before *the* American Revolution.

Sometimes Indian Runners carried heroic messages, and sometimes they tried to stop foolish slaughter. In 1790, the Creeks and the Choctaws, in an attempt to decide who had the rights to trap beaver on a pond of the Noxubee River in Mississippi, played winner-take-all "bump hips," the game that became lacrosse. As the game was often played in those days, there were hundreds to a side, and the goals were miles apart. The brawling contest soon became a bloody riot; hundreds might have died except for the speed of couriers who brought the head Chiefs to settle the dispute.

In 1890, Runners made their way to Washington, D.C., to tell the Indian version of the massacre at Wounded Knee. More than a hundred Indians, including many women and children, were killed at the Pine Ridge Reservation in South Dakota when U.S. cavalry troopers began firing into the spiritual gathering called "Ghost Dancing."

Indian athletes competed against whites, and because Indians had been hyped by newspaper reporters and cavalrymen as such powerful savages, it was big news when a white athlete beat an Indian. In 1844, in Hoboken, New Jersey, 30,000 whites cheered the New York carpenter who beat John Steeprock, a Seneca, in a $1,000 long-distance run. The sportswriter who covered the story declared the victory a triumph of white superiority.

Tom Longboat, an Onondaga (known as "The Bronze Mercury" when he won the 1907 Boston Marathon), and Louis Tewanima, a Hopi, ran in the 1908 Olympics. Ellison ("Tarzan") Brown won the Boston in 1936, and then went on to the Berlin Olympics as a member of the U.S. team. In 1964, Billy Mills, an Oglala Sioux, became the first American to win the 10,000-meter Olympic championship. There were fine major-league baseball players as Louis Sockalexis (it is said that the Cleveland Indians were named after him); Charles Bender, who was elected to the Hall of Fame; John Meyers; and Allie Reynolds.

But the most famous Indian athlete, and perhaps the greatest all-around male athlete in American history, was more than a sporting hero, and his victories were more than marks in a record book.

Jim Thorpe was a spirit of his time, a symbol of a country flexing its muscles in the world arena, a person who would not be beaten down; he was an athletic pioneer, but he also followed a path blazed by centuries of Runners for the Nation. The message he carried was his own story.

1

The graceful, restless boy Bright Path had hair as black and glistening as a raven's wing. His eyes were merry and bold. His jutting chin was square and strong. The old people watched him roam the reservation and reminded each other that this boy carried the blood of Black Hawk, their legendary warrior chief. The boy was half white, and his parents, the Thorpes, called him Jim more often than they called him Bright Path. But the old people filled the boy's head with tales of his great-uncle, who had led them against United States soldiers in the most painful, the proudest time in their history.

The Black Hawk War was short and bloody, a disaster for the Sac and Fox Nation. The natives lost the land they farmed and hunted along

the Mississippi River in what is now Illinois and
Iowa.

The war began in 1832 after some members
of the Nation sold land to the white American
government without permission of the Sac and
Fox council, which had ruled that land was not
an individual's to sell—all the land belonged to
all the people together. There were reports that
the sellers had been bribed with whiskey.

The Nation split. Some argued for peaceful
acceptance of what had unfortunately happened; after all, the U.S. Army had the fire-
power. These people were considered sellouts
by others, who begged their most famous com-
bat veteran, Black Hawk, to lead their resis-
tance.

Black Hawk, black-haired, jut-jawed, was
wary of more battle. He had fought alongside
Tecumseh, the visionary Shawnee leader who
had tried to unite all American natives into one
great army. Black Hawk knew that the troopers
had the guns and that too many Indians were
ready to make a separate peace. But in the end,
he listened to the war drums and fought for his
homeland.

The great Sac and Fox chief Black Hawk died a half century before Jim was born, but old-timers on the reservation saw the warrior's pride in the boy's eyes and his wiry strength in the boy's body. They believed Jim was a blood descendent.

Even though he was betrayed by allies who promised assistance, and hampered by mutiny and conflict in his own camp, Black Hawk won enough battles to scare whites and become the villain of newspaper stories that pressured the U.S. Army into an all-out attack. Troops on steamboats shot men, women and children hiding on the shores and small islands of the Mississippi. Finally, after hundreds of warrior and civilian Sac and Fox were slaughtered at the Battle of Bad Axe, their former friends, the Winnebagos, captured Black Hawk and turned him over to the whites.

These were critical times for Americans of color. In a close vote in 1832, the Virginia legislature defeated a proposal to emancipate black slaves. It was a turning point in the gathering movement to abolish slavery; other slave states tightened rules against freeing and educating blacks.

In his history *Custer Died for Your Sins*, Vine Deloria, Jr., wrote: "Because the Negro labored, he was considered a draft animal. Because the Indian occupied large areas of land, he was considered a wild animal."

Attitudes were being formed that have lasted to this day, that would affect even the way people treated black and Indian athletes; it would certainly affect the boy Bright Path when he became famous. He would be seen as physically superhuman but mentally and morally subhuman.

Ironically, his ancestor Black Hawk showed himself far superior to his captors; while they exhibited him as a kind of exotic beast, he left behind some remarkable interviews. He said:

> *An Indian who is as bad as a white man could not live in our Nation; he would be put to death and eaten by the wolves. The white men are bad schoolmasters; they carry false looks and deal in false actions; they smile in the face of the poor Indian to cheat him; they shake him by the hand to gain his confidence, to make him drunk, to deceive him, to ruin his wife. . . . We are not safe. We live in danger. We are becoming like them; hypocrites and liars, adulterers, lazy drones; all talkers and no workers. . . .*

By the time Black Hawk died in 1838, the Sac and Fox had been moved to a reservation on the prairie farmlands of Kansas. It was here, in 1842, that an Irish American from Connecticut, Hiram G. Thorpe, the grandfather of Bright Path, turned up looking for work.

The Bureau of Indian Affairs, a government agency staffed mostly by white men, ran the reservations, doling out land payments to the Indians and giving out jobs. Hiram was hired to be the reservation blacksmith. He married No-ten-quah, Wind Woman, believed to be Black Hawk's niece. They had six children.

Because he was white, Hiram G. Thorpe was probably better treated by the Indian agents than were the Sac and Fox, who resented the agents, their rules and the boarding schools they established to "civilize" the "savages." The schools were free; attendance was compulsory. Many Indian families tried to keep their children at home, afraid they would lose touch with their Indian roots, forget their customs and language, stop respecting their elders. But Hiram G. Thorpe, being white, was less concerned with Indian roots than with getting ahead in a white-controlled world. He insisted that his children attend the government schools to learn to read and write English. His son, Hiram P., felt the same way. Hiram P. was Bright Path's father.

The same year Black Hawk died, 1838, the Cherokees were forced off their eastern homelands to make way for white settlers and gold miners. One of every four Cherokees died from cold, hunger or disease on the wintry trek to the western reservations. No wonder they called it "The Trail of Tears."

Within a few years, the U.S. government decided that the Kansas reservation on which they had dumped the Sac and Fox was too good for them; white families moving west needed the land. The Sac and Fox would have to clear out. This was standard practice: Despite signed treaties, Indians were routinely evicted from their homes whenever white business interests wanted their land for lumber, farms, wild game, minerals, housing space. Toward the end of the nineteenth century, the U.S. government didn't even bother bribing Chiefs or getting them drunk enough to sign bad treaties; it just took the land.

The Sac and Fox Nation was dispersed. Some families found ways to stay in Kansas, while others wound their way back to the original homelands along the Mississippi and moved in with local tribes. The most adventurous, including the Thorpes, set out for Indian Territory, in what is now Oklahoma.

Hiram P. Thorpe grew up as raw and hard as the frontier, a top rider, hunter, fighter, drinker. He had a short temper and a big heart. He liked to invite his neighbors over for summer picnics behind the family cabin. Years later, Jim Thorpe would remember sitting in the cool twilight with the other children as the men raced horses and wrestled. Hiram was astonishingly quick and strong and daring. The games grew fierce, and Hiram usually won.

Hiram became a trader and sold whiskey to other Indians. This was illegal. Heavy drinking was already a serious problem in many Indian communities. If Hiram was as greedy as most traders, he probably watered the booze and added spices and tobacco juice to give it bite. It was called "firewater."

Hiram fathered at least nineteen children. His third wife, Charlotte Vieux, was also of "mixed blood," the large, strong daughter of a wealthy merchant of French descent and a Potawatomie woman. A devout Roman Catholic, Charlotte demanded that her children be baptized and attend Mass.

On May 22, 1887, she gave birth to twin boys. Disease was rampant and medicine scarce in Indian Territory (now Oklahoma)—several years earlier, Hiram and Charlotte's twin baby girls had died—but Jim and Charlie seemed healthy and strong.

Moments after James Francis Thorpe was born, his mother glanced out the window as the morning sun cut a trail of light toward the cabin door. That's how the world's greatest athlete got his Indian name: Wa-tho-huck, Bright Path.

2

"Extermination" is the battle cry now.
—THE NEW YORK TIMES

Wa-tho-huck was an optimistic name for a Native American born near the end of the nineteenth century. White America was pushing west, clearing the land to lay railroad track, dig mines, build cities. Many whites considered Indians to be merely an annoying, even dangerous, form of wildlife in the way of growth and profit.

Newspapers and cheap magazines were filled with fantasies of the "bloodthirsty Redskins" who roamed "wild" in the western paradise, worshipping birds and kidnapping white children after murdering their parents. Imagine the readers back east, many of them immigrants from Europe crammed into tiny rooms in crowded cities, scrabbling to survive by working in locked sweatshops and filthy factories. How could they understand the lives of the Thorpes, also working hard to survive, but on vast stretches of land under a big sky? No wonder so many otherwise decent Americans had no argument with local policies on the "Indian problem," which at one time included a $500 reward in Arizona for each "buck Indian's scalp."

"This reward system," *The New York Times* explained to its readers,

> *while it may seem savage and brutal to the Northern and Eastern sentimentalist, is looked upon in this section as the only means possible of ridding Arizona of the murderous Apache. . . .*
>
> *From time immemorial all border countries have offered rewards for bear and wolf scalps and other animals that destroyed the pioneer's stock or molested his family. . . . 'Extermination' is the battle cry now. . . .*

Actually, the so-called "exterminationists" were a small minority, and many white Americans did protest the inhumane treatment of natives. But most whites were conditioned to believe that Indians were a subhuman species who would die out because their time was over. Many politicians, business leaders and homesteaders believed in the "humane" way of wiping out the Indians, and that was to turn them into coppery-tinted white people—shorthaired, English speaking, churchgoing. Although the Indian school movement included exploiters who thought the savages could be tamed into cheap labor—maids, farmhands—for local settlers, the best of the schools were run by serious educators who thought the Indians' "native intelligence" could be productively channeled.

As more schools were set up, and more settlers and financiers poured into Indian Territory to gear up for Oklahoma statehood, Indians grew more concerned that their old ways would be completely forgotten and that the strength of the Indian community, extended families taking care of their own, would be destroyed.

Hiram and Charlotte apparently tried to give their children the best of both Indian and white cultures; they made sure they could read and write English, but also know about their Indian customs and languages. In later years, Jim would be able to move easily in both worlds.

Jim and Charlie, inseparable friends in the way twins often are, also learned the skills and games their father had mastered. They spent long days hunting and fishing, and some nights Hiram would take them deep into the woods so they could learn to live off the land. Jim became a good trapper and sometimes would disappear for a day or two alone, hunting and wandering through the forest.

They learned Indian games such as "fox and geese," a contest like jacks, and "crooked path," which was like "follow the leader." Jim and Charlie heard stories about the Indian Runners, those first great athletes of America, and about the old days when hundreds to a side played the ball game called "tewaarathon" by the Hau-denosaunee (Iroquois) and "baggataway" by the Algonquins, the game the French would later name "lacrosse" because the shape of the "otchi," or stick, reminded them of a bishop's crozier.

But because Hiram and Charlotte wanted their children to survive in both worlds, they sent the six-year-old twins to the nearest free In-

The game was called "bump hips" by the Iroquois, who believed it was a gift from the Creator. In early days, hundreds played on a side and the field might be miles long. A game played by many Indian Nations, it was the first team sport many Europeans ever saw. The French named it "lacrosse" because they thought the stick resembled a bishop's staff.

dian Agency boarding school, to learn "white ways." Charlie, smaller, darker and more reserved than his brother, was a careful student who earned high grades. Jim, energetic and playful, mainly excelled at recess.

The school was twenty-five miles away, and the students—more than fifty children of different ages and from different tribes—lived in dormitories. Girls and boys were separated. They studied reading and writing, arithmetic, geography and history (the white man's version, from the Pilgrims on). Afternoons were spent in the woodworking or tailor shops, or doing farm chores.

Robert Wheeler, in his biography of Thorpe *Pathway to Glory,* quotes one of Jim's classmates, Art Wakolee:

> *It took us a long time to learn our lessons in kindergarten because most of the teachers had very little patience with the Indian children. Some of the teachers were kind while others were very mean. We got a licking many times when we could not spell a simple word. As a result, we could not learn very much because most of us were afraid of our teacher.*

Before they learned the white ways, however, they had to unlearn their Indian ways.

"They told us Indian ways were bad," Sun Elk, a Taos Pueblo, remembered of his days at the famous Carlisle Indian School in Pennsylvania in Peter Nabokov's *Native American Testimony*. "They said we must get civilized. I remember that word too. It means 'be like the white man.' I am willing to be like the white man but I did not believe Indian ways were wrong."

Maybe Jim did not believe it either, or maybe he was just bored in school; his backside ached on the hard wooden chair; voices droned stale facts and figures into his throbbing head while outside the window the sun shone down on the grass and the trees. Whatever the reason, Jim was no teacher's pet. He shot at flies with rubber bands, did somersaults in class, farted at the teacher.

He escaped several times, sneaking out of the three-story brick dorm and shedding his uniform as he ran home to an angry Hiram, who would throw his sobbing son in the wagon and drive him back to school. Once, after an escape, Hiram returned to his farm after dropping Jim off at the school only to find Jim had escaped again and run the twenty-five miles to beat his father home.

Jim eventually settled down. His older brothers encouraged him to stay in school, and he began to enjoy some of the games they played in their free time, especially a new game that was becoming increasingly popular throughout the country, a Colonial cousin of cricket called "baseball." Jim was a deft fielder with a powerful throwing arm, speedy on the bases and a slugger at bat. The game had started as an upper-class sport, but immigrant groups took it over, and by the time Jim was playing, there were professional leagues and fans were arguing whether German Americans or Irish Americans were more "naturally suited" to the game.

But it was Jim's love for his brother Charlie, not baseball, that kept him in school. The twins were very different, yet they understood each other in ways no one else could. Jim, robust and adventurous, and Charlie, thoughtful and calm, seemed to complement each other. Jim protected Charlie from the bullies. Charlie helped Jim with his schoolwork. They shared secrets, they kept each other's spirits up.

Then pneumonia and smallpox swept through the school in the spring of 1897. Charlie died. Nothing could console Jim. Almost ten,

Bright Path grew dark and sad. Even the games were no longer fun. He ran away again.

When Jim was eleven, Hiram decided to send him to a distant boarding school. He is supposed to have said to his son: "I'm going to send you so far, you will never find your way home again."

3

I want him to go make something of himself, for he cannot do it here.

—HIRAM P. THORPE

Homesick and mourning Charlie, Jim was twelve when he arrived at the Haskell Indian School outside Lawrence, Kansas, in 1899. Haskell was renowned for its ethic of work, discipline and, most of all, assimilation into "white ways." Like all the government-run Indian boarding schools, Haskell was free. After Carlisle, in Pennsylvania, Haskell was the most famous Indian school in the country.

Jim kept his dark suit clean and his buttons shiny as he trudged from class in the morning to the shops in the afternoon, learning to bake bread, sew clothes and wire electricity. The rules were strict: no roughhousing, no tardiness, no romance between students. And never, ever, speak in your native language.

Students from the same tribe were not allowed to room together. Often, youngsters would return to their reservations after years at Haskell unable to talk with their families. Even if they relearned the old language, they were treated like aliens.

As the Pueblo Chiefs told Sun Elk's father: "He has no hair. He has no blankets. He cannot even speak our language and he has a strange smell. He is not one of us."

When Jim arrived at Haskell, the sports craze was football, which had begun thirty years before as a brutal, sometimes deadly game played at elite Eastern colleges. (President Theodore Roosevelt called for safety measures after his son was knocked unconscious in a game between Harvard and Yale.)

As football's popularity spread, so did a national debate; some said it built character, others that it taught violence. Its language was military; after all the quarterback was a "field general" and teams "crushed," "routed" and "demolished" their "foes."

What kind of character football builds is a question people still argue today. But in 1899,

By 1880 football was an established college sport, less organized than today but at least as brutal. Then as now, some people thought it had no place in higher education, while others saw it as a great way for less-privileged students to get ahead.

as Americans began to imagine themselves the greatest nation on earth, football was seen as a fierce and dramatic game that only Americans played. It was easy for Jim to catch the football fever. Haskell encouraged the sport as another way to turn Indians into Americans.

The hero of Haskell was Chauncey Archiquette, star quarterback and honor student. Chauncey shouted out pointers from the sidelines as Jim and the other younger boys fought over a rag-stuffed cloth ball, crashing into each other, mimicking the stances and moves of their varsity models.

For Jim, football was recess in a long, strange year of so many new faces and new routines. He missed Charlie, and he missed home. He kept himself busy with chores and schoolwork. He had just begun to settle into Haskell when he received word that his father had been badly wounded in a hunting accident.

Jim walked right off the Haskell grounds in his work clothes and hopped on a freight train, only the train was going in the wrong direction. When he realized his mistake, he jumped off and walked for two weeks back the other way.

He returned home to a healed and raging
Hiram. "How could you run away again!" his
father exploded, hurling his son to the ground.
Hiram and Jim felt betrayed by each other; the
father because his son had walked away from
his future, and the son because his father re-
acted so angrily to his concerned love.

Jim hung around for a while, but the tension
was thick. In the small house, Jim felt in the way
of his younger brother and sister. His mother,
Charlotte, was pregnant again. He helped with
the chores and sometimes attended the one-
room public school that had just opened nearby.
But he was restless and bored.

One morning, Jim headed out for the Texas
border. There were no uniforms or school bells
out in cattle country, just hard work. Jim built
fences and broke horses, skills Hiram had taught
him. He was thirteen, scrawny but strong, and
he was out on his own.

After a while, he grew tired of the range life.
The days were long, the nights were cold and
he was surrounded by lonely men who worked
to exhaustion for liquor money. Being a cowboy
was never glamorous work. He saved his wages

to buy a team of horses that he rode home and gave to Hiram as a peace offering and a way of showing his father that he was now a man who could take care of himself, who didn't need to go to school. Hiram invited Jim to stay and help with the family.

But the family had changed. While Jim was away, his mother had died in childbirth, along with the baby. Hiram soon married his fourth wife, a white woman named Julia. It was crowded in the house, and the relationship with his new stepmother was strained.

One of his few pleasures those days back in Oklahoma was baseball, marathon games played out in the fields on Saturdays or before supper during the week. Jim's months on the range had paid off; he was incredibly strong for his age. Recruiters from semipro teams and colleges came to see him blast the ball over barn roofs, fire pinpoint throws to home from deep center or pitch humming fastballs. He was only fifteen, and raw, but also smart and talented. He had a gift for games.

Hiram dreamed of something better than prairie baseball for Jim, and he wrote a letter to

the Carlisle Indian School in Pennsylvania asking for their help. It was even farther away than
Haskell, and more prestigious. It was probably
on the basis of Hiram's plea, which must have
touched the school's sense of purpose, that Jim
was accepted.

"I want him to go make something of himself," Hiram wrote, "for he cannot do it here."

4

> I believe in immersing the Indians in our civilization, and when we get them under holding them there until they are thoroughly soaked.
>
> —RICHARD HENRY PRATT

On Jim's first day at the Carlisle Indian School, in early February 1904, he and the other new students were herded into the barbershop for short haircuts. For some, it meant losing long traditional braids they had worn all their lives, symbols of their tribal identity. For Jim, who had been through all this before, it was probably just a haircut.

The students were issued military-style uniforms. Afterward, teachers handed out slates for the first test: Write your name. This meant, of course, your Christian name. If you didn't have one, the school would make one up for you. Maybe it should have been called a *de*-Indian school.

The Indian schools' first step in turning their young students into red-skinned white folks was to cut their hair and put them in uniforms. This is what a group of Chiricuhua Apaches from Florida looked like when they arrived at Carlisle in November of 1883.

Finally, boys and girls were separated and organized into military formations, with student officers in charge of marching them through the Carlisle campus, an old Army compound of abandoned barracks, to the main parade grounds, where Colonel Richard Henry Pratt, the founder and principal, addressed them.

Jim and his classmates had probably already heard stories about him from the older students. Pratt had been a famous Indian fighter. He might have hunted many of their relatives back

And this is what they looked like four months later.

in the 1860's and 1870's. Pratt had helped train
and lead the Tenth Cavalry, the so-called Buf-
falo Soldiers, African-American troopers com-
manded by white officers. In 1879, he had
opened Carlisle; there were now about one
thousand students.

As Pratt explained to his new students, his
experiences with his own black soldiers and
their Indian scouts, and with captured Indian
warriors, had convinced him that all people
were created equal, that whites were not superior to blacks or reds. He believed that people of
color, especially Native Americans, had not only

been treated unjustly but underrated as well.

Indians, he told the new students, because of their intelligence, character and adaptability, could flourish in the white world if given the chance. And the purpose of Carlisle was to give them that chance—their only hope of survival, according to Pratt.

"I believe in immersing the Indians in our civilization," he had written, "and when we get them under holding them there until they are thoroughly soaked. There is a great amount of sentiment among Indian teachers but in the work of breaking up Indian customs there is no room for sentiment."

Jim was no stranger to these notions—his old schools had been based on them, too—but he braced himself for an especially grueling first year. The awkwardness and uncertainty of being a new boy were familiar, but now there was the added intensity of this Pratt and his obsession for assimilation.

The rules were stricter here and the punishment for breaking them more severe, too. Students were kept occupied with class and chores all the time and very rarely allowed to leave the campus. Even though some students were in their late teens and early twenties, sex was outlawed: Caught, you were sent home in disgrace.

In some ways, life was easier at Carlisle for Jim than for many of the other youngsters; he was physically strong and tough-minded, he had survived on his own out in the world and he was half white—there was less Indian that had to be drummed out of him.

Yet, for some of those same reasons, Carlisle life was harsher on Jim; he knew what freedom was—he had always rebelled against authority—and it must have been hard for him to accept the Carlisle credo that there was something wrong with him, his Indian side, that needed to be scraped away.

Later that year, his father, Hiram, died from a snakebite. Sad and lonely, Jim decided to stick it out in his new home.

One activity at Carlisle that Jim hated were the "outings." Colonel Pratt believed that to truly understand white ways, the students needed contact with whites in a close, daily environment. They were sent off for months at a time to live with and work for local families. It would be a chance to perfect their English and learn how to deal with whites. Despite a screening process to make sure people wouldn't exploit the students, there were some reports of abuse by farmers who saw the Carlisle students only as a source of cheap labor.

Jim despised cooking and cleaning, and one time he just quit an outing assignment and returned to Carlisle. He spent a few days in the guardhouse for that. Another time, the outing family felt so sorry for him, they requested he be returned to school. But back at school, Jim was faced with textbooks, which he didn't much like either. There was only one solution: The "Athletic Boys" of Carlisle never had to go on outings, and their exploits on the field cut them slack in the classroom.

Years before Jim's arrival at Carlisle, Pratt had realized that the school would always need more money than it got from the government, and favorable publicity—there were too many people who thought teaching "savages" was a waste of time and taxes. Pratt knew one sure way to get cash and ink—winning sports teams. It's a technique that many universities use today. By the time Jim arrived at Carlisle, Pratt had already picked the man to help keep his dream alive.

Glenn Warner, a big, young, gruff coach, was legendary at the school. He had been called "Pop" since his college days at Cornell, when he played football years past his eligibility. He was relentless in his drive to make Carlisle a football powerhouse. He could be nasty, abusive and profane. Once he hit a player for making a mistake. But he could also be very kind, and he respected the players and their abilities.

Indian athletes on the whole have always been less willing to be yelled at than most white athletes (even now, rather than complain about a coach's behavior, they will simply leave the team), but they are also more willing to put aside the quest for personal glory for the good of the group. According to both Indian and non-Indian coaches, Indian athletes tend to take criticism poorly, but because they have been trained as observers, they learn very quickly. These are cultural differences that good coaches learn to accept and even use. Pop Warner was a good coach—he toned down his foul language and took advantage of his players' specialness, which happened to fit his own playful inventiveness. Pop's ideas were the wave of the future in a new game that did not yet have the technological precision of the NFL today. Pop would go on to coach for many years at major universities—Carlisle was his laboratory.

Pop came up with the "Indian block," in which a player led with his hips and used his whole body to hit, instead of just his shoulders. Pop taught his passers to throw perfect spirals. From discarded wood and cloth he built the first blocking sleds, and drilled his linemen in blocking techniques. He spent hours in the Carlisle shops designing new kinds of padding and gear.

Warner's most notorious play was the "hidden ball trick." During one game, the Carlisle team formed a giant wedge to receive a kickoff. Hidden from the opposing team but not from the giggles and shouts in the stands, the receiver slipped the ball into a special pouch sewn into the back of a blocker's jersey. The blocker practically walked in for a touchdown while the other team searched frantically for the ball.

Eventually, the play was outlawed, but Pop didn't mind. Football was still a young game with flabby rules, and he had plenty of other tricks up his sleeve, most of which he invented out of necessity; in the days in which a 200-pound lineman was considered huge, Carlisle players rarely weighed more than 160.

Jim, who was small for his age as a teenager, was about 5 feet 5 inches and 120 pounds when he arrived at Carlisle not quite seventeen years old. Nevertheless, he played intramural football that year, on the tailor-shop team. Like everyone else, he worshipped the varsity players from afar. But it was track and field that first got him noticed, three years later.

One spring twilight on his way to a game, in 1907, Jim walked by the high-jump pit and sat down to watch the varsity jumpers practice. They set the bar higher and higher until one by one none of them could clear it. Jim, still in his bulky work overalls, asked for a try. The varsity jumpers laughed and shrugged.

He leaped the bar with ease. Nobody said a word, and Jim walked away. The next afternoon one of the jumpers found Jim in the dining hall.

"Do you know what you did?" the jumper supposedly asked.

It's not hard to imagine this cocky young Jim Thorpe as a jock hero today.

"What?" For a moment Jim might have been afraid he would be punished or, worse, sent on an outing.

"You broke the school record."

When Pop, who was the track coach as well as football coach and athletic director, heard the news, he issued Jim a team uniform. He asked his star, Albert Exendine, to whip Jim into

The 1909 Carlisle track team poses for its group portrait. That's Pop in the suit and tie, and Jim, already twenty-two years old, seated fourth from the left, under Pop's shoulder.

shape. The two became close friends, even after Jim's first season, when he broke all of Albert's records. Jim and Albert became the best known of all the Athletic Boys.

But what Jim really wanted was to play varsity football.

5

Nobody tackles Jim.
—JIM THORPE

One afternoon in the fall of 1907, so the legend goes, Jim marched to the varsity football practice in a borrowed uniform two sizes too large and asked to try out for the team. Everyone chuckled except Pop Warner, who shouted something like "Take that uniform off!" He would not have wanted his new track star to get banged around.

"I want to play," Jim might have said, perhaps with that tough, stubborn look in his eye that teammates later remembered.

"If that's the way you want it," said Pop, tossing Jim the first real leather football he'd ever held. He pointed to the varsity players warming up on the field. "Give them some tackling practice."

Jim strolled to one end zone, hugged the ball and took off. He had an easy lope, a distance runner's stride, and the first player to reach him leaped like a wolf on a deer. He was shocked when all he grabbed was air before he hit the ground. Jim cut and spun and stopped short, leaving the heroes of Carlisle sprawled behind him on the grass. He sprinted the last twenty yards and no one was close.

Pop was speechless as Jim trotted back to the sideline.

"Nobody tackles Jim," he said, trying not to grin.

"You can't do that again," sputtered Pop.

Of course he could. It was a little harder this time—the varsity was ready and steamed—but Jim wove his way through the entire team, dodging tacklers, wriggling out of a grasp, now and then stiff-arming someone out of his way.

What could Pop say? "Get him a uniform that fits."

That first season, Jim practiced the fundamentals: blocking and tackling, how to read the opposing team, how to bring a ballcarrier down and shake the ball loose. He practiced drop and place kicking until he could split the goal posts at every distance from nearly impossible angles.

But he didn't start right away. Carlisle was becoming a national football power behind quarterback Frank Mt. Pleasant, who had a rifle arm and a quick mind. While most teams used size and brute strength to win games that were more bar brawl than sport, Carlisle relied on what newspapers of the day described as a "wealth of marvelous plays" and "beautifully executed forward passes."

The team lost only one game that season, but it somehow got a reputation for not being tough in bad conditions like rain or snow or on a mud-soaked field. Journalists had a habit of writing that the Indians played for sheer pleasure rather than school pride, so when the weather killed the fun, they just gave up. Actually, many of their tricky plays simply didn't work on a slippery field with a wet ball.

The theories the sportswriters offered were part of the white mind-set that saw Indians as "noble savages," alternately childlike, barbaric, cunning, innocent, certainly too close to nature to be like other Americans. This attitude helped rationalize either the massacre of Indians (they were "bloodthirsty redskins") or the taking control of their land and education (they needed to be protected). It was used to justify herding them into rural ghettoes and stripping away their language, clothes, religion.

This attitude made it impossible to treat Indians as fellow citizens, to respect their culture or to trust them to make their own decisions about their lives. In sports, this attitude made it impossible to see teams from Carlisle as hardworking, well-trained, motivated units. It was easier to see them as peaceful war parties of animalistic grace and power.

There is an enduring myth about Jim arriving alone at an out-of-town track meet and winning every single event. A one-man varsity. It simply wasn't true, but it fit into that white misconception of the primitive superman who never needed to train. It has followed Jim Thorpe to this day, that image of a great performing animal. It was hard for people to accept an Indian as hardworking, well-conditioned, smart.

A half century later, when African-American

athletes began to dominate major-league team sports, sportswriters and sportscasters often cast them as "natural" athletes rather than products of intelligent hard work, as were white athletes. It was the same kind of attitude at work.

But as far as Coach Warner was concerned, so long as his team was becoming nationally famous and bringing in money, the sportswriters could have their fantasies. And Pop's team soon became even more of a public relations machine than Colonel Pratt could have hoped. Raggedy little Carlisle, which was not even an accredited college, was playing the big college teams—Harvard, Yale, Pennsylvania, Syracuse, Princeton, Minnesota—and not only beating them but raking in a fortune on ticket sales. Later on, after Pratt had left, there would be a scandal that closed Carlisle: Investigations would show that Pop slipped some of the money into his own pocket.

But Pop took care of his Athletic Boys. Everything was easier for Jim the moment he pulled on the jersey with the big "C" on the front. He lived in a more comfortable dorm than other students, ate more and better food

How good was the 1912 Carlisle football team? Jim, Pete Calac, a Mission Indian from California, and Joe Guyan, a Chippewa from Minnesota, were eventually inducted into the professional football Hall of Fame. It was the only time in history three players from the same college team made the Hall. That good.

and got spending money from the coach—just like at a real college. Downtown, at Mose Blumenthal's store, Jim could get a fancy suit on Pop's account, and some extra cash from Mose, who like many merchants in town was a team booster. The school's fame brought business to their stores, hotels and restaurants.

But Carlisle was not so easy for its academic honor students. Jack Newcombe, in his book about Jim Thorpe, *The Best of the Athletic Boys*, quotes a letter from Emma Newashe, a Sac and Fox girl, to her Indian agent requesting money for a dress: ". . . As I am President of the society I certainly will have to look decent. If I am not dressed as if I was at a reception why what will they think of their President? Mr. Kohlenberg just you put yourself in my place, having no parents to look after you, to send you no clothing. . . ."

It was her own money she was asking for, from the account the local Indian agent had set up for each Sac and Fox as part of the payoff for the government taking their land. The agent had control of the account, and Emma Newashe probably did not get her dress. But the athletes got all the perks they wanted, and some they may not have even known about. Pop paid off the local police to keep his boys out of jail when they sneaked off school grounds and went carousing downtown.

Jim enjoyed that winter after his first football season. He'd stroll the campus with his teammates, basking in the adulation, or go into town for drinks on the house. Pop bent school rules on alcohol for his athletes. Perhaps he felt they deserved to let off steam, they worked so hard; perhaps it was a way of keeping them—many were in their twenties—in school, another example of white men using firewater.

In spring, Jim trained hard for track. Although he never cared as much about setting records as he did about winning his event and scoring points for the team, he set a school hurdle record, the first of many.

Track teammates of Jim's included quarterback Mt. Pleasant, who was a master at the broad jump, and long-distance running champion Louis Tewanima, a Hopi from the Southwest. That summer, not long after putting on his first pair of running shoes, Tewanima placed ninth in the marathon at the 1908 Olympic Games in London.

Jim went home to Oklahoma for the summer. Ed and Adaline, his younger brother and sister, were still mourning Hiram. Jim entertained them with stories of his long leap from overalls to a varsity uniform. Jim's older half-brother, Frank, took him hunting and fishing. They shared memories of their father. Jim was twenty-one years old, and he began to find comfort in his family.

Then it was time to head back to Carlisle and suit up for his first big season.

6

By 1908, Jim's name dominated school cheers, press clippings and football award lists. Many of the eleven games Carlisle won that season were decided at the last minute by Jim's clutch kicking.

There were bitter defeats, too; The 17–0 loss to Harvard, that training school for millionaires and presidents, was seen by Carlisle as another humiliation at the hands of the privileged white establishment.

In the grueling 6–6 tie with Pennsylvania that Jim would later call the toughest game of his life, he missed several easy field goals before breaking loose for a long run at the very end. Such heroics led to Jim's selection as a third-team All-America.

There wasn't much time for classes. As they do today, major college teams practiced and traveled with the intensity of professionals. Jim and his friends tried to catch up on their school-work during the winter, but they knew that so long as they won, teachers and administrators would never flunk them out.

Jim became even more valuable to Carlisle that spring, when he won nearly every track and field event he entered and, in his first start for the Carlisle baseball team, pitched a no-hitter.

When the school year ended, hungry for a change of scene, Jim followed Carlisle class-mates Possum Powell and Jesse Young Deer down to the North Carolina tobacco country, a hotbed of semipro ball. Jim signed on as an infielder with Rocky Mount of the East Carolina League. Although playing for money violated college and amateur athletic rules, it was com-mon practice, and officials looked the other way. Many college athletes played under false names—including, the story goes, future Presi-dent Dwight D. Eisenhower, a West Point half-back who roamed minor-league outfields as "Wilson."

For reasons that have never been fully explained, Jim played under his own name. Did he think he'd never be caught? Was he too honest to lie? Or, most likely, did he think it didn't matter because he had decided not to return to Carlisle? In any case, Jim's speed alone made him famous in semipro ball. One Fayetteville shortstop remembered bending down to field a hard grounder only to see Jim already blazing past first base.

The league was a mix of journeymen and college boys. Jim earned about twenty-five dollars a week, not a luxurious salary but enough to live comfortably. Local kids often gathered outside the hotels of their favorite players and carried their mitts and bats to the park. Jim was a favorite, and he loved the friendly, small-town attention and the free time without schoolwork, assemblies, chores, rules. After a while, he wired Carlisle to say he wouldn't be back. He asked his local Indian agent for some of the money in his account. It was grudgingly sent. When the baseball season ended, Jim went home to Oklahoma and found work as a hired hand. He was twenty-two years old.

Meanwhile, the Carlisle football team struggled through the 1909 season. When Jim visited the school for Christmas, Pop begged him to stay for the track season, but Jim refused; as much as he enjoyed the comradeship and the attention, he was tired of school and rules. Out in the world, he was a gifted athlete being paid for his skills, who could live the way he wanted, come and go as he pleased. In the late spring of 1910 he signed up for another season with the Rocky Mount team. Again he returned to Oklahoma for the winter. He began to feel as though he was drifting aimlessly through his life. He worked hard and he drank hard. He began to miss the security and order of school life.

And Oklahoma was changing, booming with more white settlers, more new businesses, and more hostility toward Indians, who were viewed as being in the way of progress. There was discrimination in jobs, and nasty remarks on the street.

Motion pictures were the newest craze, and one of their major action subjects was the West. The "good" cowboys almost always won. The prevailing movie attitude was "the only good Indian is a dead Indian."

That year a Chippewa delegation sent a letter to President Taft protesting the depiction of Indians by Hollywood as drunks, fools, cannibals, rapists and savages. Long after the battle for territory had ended, the battle for human rights and ethnic identity raged on. And still does.

Maybe Jim began yearning for a place where Indians were treated with dignity, even if they were being de-Indianized; a place where he was a hero, even in the downtown stores. He seemed ready to leave Oklahoma one afternoon when he bumped into Albert Exendine, in town visiting friends. Jim's old track mentor had earned a law degree after leaving Carlisle and was now coaching at a small college. When Jim admitted he hadn't been up to much lately, Ex suggested he go back and finish school. Play some more football. He noticed how much bigger Jim was now, more muscular.

"They wouldn't want me there now," said Jim, according to Jack Newcombe's book.

"You bet they would," said Ex. He dragged Jim to a telegraph office, and they sent Carlisle a wire requesting Jim's readmission.

Academic officials weren't sure if he was

"worthy" of an education. Jim's dropping out had disappointed them. And he was, after all, twenty-four years old.

But Coach Pop Warner was thrilled at the chance for another powerhouse football team, and maybe even a trip to the Stockholm Olympics that summer with Jim and Louis Tewanima. Warner convinced the administration that Carlisle could not *afford* to refuse Jim. After all, hadn't he always been "worthy" enough to sell tickets?

Pop was not only an innovative coach but a pioneer in the field of sports public relations. His staff hyped the team into a national powerhouse, and during the 1911 season it dubbed Jim "greatest all-around athlete in the world." The label stuck even before it was proven true.

In football, he was a wonder. Jim's most feared tactic during those games was a punt kicked so high that he could race downfield before the ball landed, in plenty of time for a bone-crushing tackle or even a recovery and touchdown. After one of the mighty Thorpe exhibitions that fans came to expect every time he played, *The Pittsburgh Dispatch* wrote: "This person was a host in himself. Tall and sinewy, as

Pop Warner was a model for the modern king-coach, who often has more power than the college president. But then as now, the coach needed "the horses," the blue-chip athletes who actually do the work. Pop's horses were Jim and Louis Tewanima, the Hopi long-distance runner.

quick as a flash and as powerful as a turbine engine, he appeared to be impervious to injury."

Quick and powerful, yes, but not impervious. An ankle sprain put him out of action for two weeks, and though not quite healed, he suited up for the game against Harvard, a chance to avenge the 1908 loss. The media buildup was intense, and nearly thirty thousand people attended the game in Cambridge.

The arrogant Harvard coach was so convinced that Carlisle was no match for his team that he didn't even bother to show up for the game, and he ordered his assistant to play only the substitutes.

By the end of the first half, Harvard led by

three points. Carlisle, losing to scrubs, got mad, got even and then got ahead on a spectacular breakaway touchdown and a couple of those towering kicks by Jim. Disobeying their absent coach, the frantic Harvard captains brought out the varsity team—the cavalry charging to save the day.

But it was too late. Nobody could bring Jim down. When his ankle finally gave out and he hobbled off the field, a stadium filled with Harvard fans let out a wild cheer. Later, the Harvard coach was quoted as saying, "I realized that he was the theoretical superplayer in flesh and blood."

Jim was a superstar. The next morning's papers hailed him as a future Hall of Famer. The team returned to Carlisle for days of dances, banquets and speeches.

It was sometime during those happy days of celebration that Jim discovered another reason to be glad he had come back to school. Her name was Iva Miller. She was eighteen years old, a pretty, popular honor student. While Jim loved to laugh and to dance, he was no social smoothy. In fact, according to Newcombe, he

Looking at this scrubby football field and these smallish young men in their old-fashioned uniforms, second-rate even for the time, one can only imagine how talented they were and how hard they worked to beat the best college teams in the country.

was considered a tacky dresser who was awkward around women. His first words to Iva were supposedly, "You're a cute little thing." But by Christmas of that year, people noticed that Jim was dressing more carefully and trying to act more suave. He was falling in love.

7

Thanks, King.
—JIM THORPE

The U.S.S. *Finland*, decorated in red, white and blue, set sail from New York on June 14, 1912, for Stockholm. It was Jim's first ocean ride, a joyous, rowdy trip, the best part of the Olympics, he would say later. With Pop coaching, Jim and Louis Tewanima trained on deck with their 150 American Olympic teammates. They spent hours every day on the cork track that circled the jumping mats and the swimming pool. There were newspaper stories that Jim snoozed in a hammock for most of the voyage. His teammates said that no one trained harder.

The Stockholm Olympics were the fifth Games, and the first that Americans took seriously. Women competed for the first time in 1912. From 1896 through 1908, rich young men from club teams were the core of the U.S.

Jim jogs on the deck of the ship that carried the American squad to the 1912 Olympic Games. Teammates said he trained as hard as anyone, but sportswriters, who preferred their fantasy of the "natural athlete," claimed he spent most of the trip snoozing in a hammock.

squad. But by 1912, Americans saw the Olympics as another way of flexing their muscles in the world arena.

The original Olympics in ancient Greece were also a stage for nationalistic muscle flexing—Athenians versus Spartans versus Macedonians—and sleazy practices. There were fixed races, performance-enhancing drugs (strychnine was used as a stimulant) and sexism—women were banned from even watching under pain of death, for the men competed naked.

When Baron de Coubertin of France reintroduced the Olympic Games in 1896, he announced his intentions of inspiring better international understanding through sport. Some historians believe his real motivation was to whip his own countrymen into better physical shape for their next war: They had recently lost the Franco-Prussian War to Germany.

Whatever the original purpose, there was no mistaking the elitism of the modern Games. Millionaires and aristocrats ran the Olympics, and only amateurs (the word is from the Latin meaning "to love," in this case, playing for love of sport rather than money) were allowed to compete. Olympic leaders wanted their event "pure" of the professionalism and commercialism of soccer, baseball and football. An athlete who had ever taken money to play sports or advertise products was barred from the Olympics for life. If it was discovered that an Olympic athlete had ever "played for pay," he or she would be stripped of medals and records.

It's doubtful if Jim was even thinking of such distinctions as amateur and professional. For him, the Olympics was a big, exciting track meet in another country, all expenses paid. There was no money for competing or even winning.

Pop had entered Jim in the two most difficult Olympic competitions: the pentathlon, which in those days consisted of the running broad jump, the javelin throw, the 200-meter dash, the discus toss and the 1500-meter run; and the decathlon, which was the pentathlon plus the 100-meter

As the U.S. Olympic track team lines up for a group picture, Jim, in a turtleneck, stares off in another direction. What is he seeing, thinking about? At 5 feet 11 inches tall, he's one of the shorter athletes.

The field events of the Olympic pentathlon and decathlon were not Jim's best, but he was strong and graceful, and was a fast learner.

dash, the pole vault, the high jump, the 110-meter hurdles, the shot put and the 400-meter run.

Although some people say the decathlon is for athletes who aren't really good enough in any one event, most people think the decathlon

winner is the best all-around athlete in the
world. The decathlon is the ultimate test of
speed, strength and stamina.

Not only did Jim win gold medals in both
events, he set a decathlon record that lasted for
sixteen years. Because training has advanced
enormously through the twentieth century,
there is no truly objective way of comparing
Jim to today's athletes; but remember that
neither Bo Jackson nor Deion Sanders, among
versatile modern stars, won the Olympic
decathlon.

Jim was humble about his accomplishments
but not surprised. "I had trained well and hard
and had confidence in my ability," he said.

Along with the gold medals, King Gustav V
of Sweden presented Jim with a valuable royal
bronze bust. Czar Nicholas II of Russia presented him with a jewel-encrusted silver chalice
in the shape of a Viking ship.

The attention Jim received was overwhelm-
ing, from the thousands on hand and the millions worldwide who followed his triumphs in
the press. Louis Tewanima's triumph, a silver
medal in the 10,000 meters against the strongest

Jim may or may not really have said "Thanks, King," when Gustav of Sweden called him the world's greatest athlete. But what would you say to a starchy old gent like this?

field ever assembled, was lost in the excitement over Jim.

Jim Thorpe was the first global sports star, the sporting ancestor of Pelé and Muhammad Ali and Michael Jordan. But he wasn't as good as his successors at controlling his image. When King Gustav placed a laurel wreath on Jim's head and the medal around his neck, the king said, "Sir, you are the greatest athlete in the world."

"Thanks, King," Jim is said to have replied. People who read that chuckled at the stereotype of the barely civilized native and the sophisticated royal. But historians are not convinced that such a conversation ever took place. It might be just another story, like the one about Jim training in a hammock on the transatlantic trip.

After exhibitions in Europe, the U.S. team returned to a ticker-tape parade in New York City. Jim rode in his own car and waved to millions of cheering fans. President Taft wrote him a letter. Owners of pro sports teams begged him to play football or baseball for them. Theater impresarios offered him big contracts to go on their stages; he could sing a few songs, dance, tell jokes, anything. Just his name on the marquee outside the theater would mean a full house inside.

But Pop convinced Jim to come back to Carlisle for one more year. Maybe he stressed loyalty to coach and school, reminded him that Iva was waiting or told him that after another good year in college football, he'd be worth even more.

8

I hope I will be partly excused by the fact that I was simply an Indian schoolboy. . . .

—JIM THORPE

A friend of Thorpe's, Pete Calac, who played at Carlisle and later in the pros, recalled: "Jim never acted like he was better than any of us, in spite of his great fame. He always tried to be just one of the guys."

But it was Jim who made "the guys" the team to beat. He was a blur, kicking goals from outlandish distances, crunching and juking his way through entire defenses, taking daring, crowd-pleasing, calculated risks. Like all great athletes, he knew exactly what his body could do.

Pop would have benched anyone else foolish enough not to down the ball in the Lehigh end zone, but there wasn't much he could say when Jim shook loose from the half dozen tacklers swarming over him and bolted 110 yards for a touchdown. Jim was twenty-five years old at that time, and probably at the peak of his speed and conditioning. While he was good sized for a running back of his era—just under 6 feet tall, about 180 pounds—his rocket-burst runs were powered by muscles developed in track and field.

The most anticipated game that 1912 season was against West Point. It was billed as the classic match of Indian speed and savvy against Army size and power. Looking back now, it seems like a metaphor: a team of future Army officers, symbolic sons of Custer and all the Indian fighters, against the symbolic sons of the warrior Chiefs, doing battle with a football instead of a cannonball. But that might not have been in any of the players' minds. On both sides they were jocks getting a free education at a government school and playing their hearts out for coach and teammates.

There was no doubt football filled Jim's head that day. Jim set up touchdowns for his teammates and scored one himself on a brilliant run, only to have it called back on an offside penalty.

Two cadets tried to take Jim out with a high-low tackle, but Jim pulled up in time to watch them knock each other into a daze and stagger out of the game. One of them was "Ike" Eisenhower, the future president.

Tired from a hard win, the Carlisle Indians lost their next game against a mediocre University of Pennsylvania team, but they won the rest. After a game against the YMCA eleven of Worcester, Massachusetts, Pop decided to let his team stay in the New England town for a few days of recuperation and training.

One day, a young editor for *The Worcester Telegram*, Roy Johnson, came by to watch Carlisle work out. He was chatting on the sidelines with Charley Clancy, a baseball manager. When Jim jogged by, Clancy pointed excitedly: "Hey, I know that guy!"

"Of course you do," Johnson probably said. "That's Jim Thorpe."

Clancy explained that he had known Jim a few years back, when he'd managed a club down in the Carolinas. Jim was that fast kid on the Rocky Mount team.

Johnson's heart skipped a beat. This was hot

news. He could imagine the headline: "Greatest Amateur Athlete in the World Played for Money!" It was the kind of scoop that makes a reporter's career.

Johnson was in a dilemma. He didn't want to hurt Jim. He believed the amateur rules were hypocritical; they favored rich athletes who didn't need to make a living. And, like many people, he felt the rules were unfairly strict. (Today, when most major Olympic athletes get paid, it's hard to understand what agony Roy Johnson must have gone through, weighing the pros and cons of breaking his big story.)

Meanwhile, Jim announced that the Thanksgiving game against Brown University, the last of the season, would also be his final college football appearance. Jim's teammates and fans wanted him to go out with a bang, and he obliged with three touchdowns and two field goals in a swirling blizzard. When the 32–0 victory ended, even the referee was flabbergasted.

"The greatest football player, ever" was all the referee could manage to say. Every newspaper agreed. Jim was selected first team All-America for the second year in a row.

Jim went back to Oklahoma for the holidays and returned to Carlisle, as he had so many times before, a modest and casual hero who tried to take seriously his role as a model. He gave inspirational speeches to the younger students in a pleasant, straightforward style. He made an effort to catch up on some schoolwork; the poet Marianne Moore, who taught at Carlisle early in her career, remembered him that last year as polite and intelligent, but because of the demands of sports usually unprepared in class and often absent.

He even won a school dance contest. He brought the first prize, a chocolate cake, back to the dorm. Jim was always generous with his possessions and his money.

And then everything changed. Roy Johnson, who believed it was his journalistic duty, broke his big story in January 1913, using the information from Charley Clancy. At a hearing before the Amateur Athletic Union (AAU), Clancy denied everything he had said to Johnson, and Pop, desperate to cover for himself, lied and said he never knew his athletes played summer ball. Later, when players from the Carolina leagues confirmed the truth, Jim was left dangling to take all the blame.

Pop wrote a letter and persuaded Jim to copy it over in his own hand. Warner read it as Jim's words at the AAU hearing.

I hope I will be partly excused by the fact that I was simply an Indian schoolboy and I did not know all about such things. In fact I did not know I was doing wrong because I was doing what I knew several other college men had done. . . . I have always liked sport and only played or ran races for the fun of things and never to earn money.

The letter was an admission of guilt and got everyone off the hook except Jim. The U.S. Olympic Committee, Carlisle and Pop Warner were all cleared of charges that they had known Jim played pro ball and yet had still allowed him to compete as an amateur. The bust of King Gustav and the Russian czar's chalice were returned to the International Olympic Committee, and the gold medals, which Jim had given to Pop for safekeeping, were awarded to

The gold medals Jim had to return after the 1912 Olympics weren't gold-plated, as they are today, but he had cherished them as priceless souvenirs of the time when he was the best in the world.

the second-place finishers. The name James Thorpe was stricken from Olympic record books. It was as if the flashing cameras, the cheering fans, the astonished athletes, were all an Indian fable and Jim had never been in Stockholm at all.

Was justice served? Even at the time, many people didn't think so. The fact that Jim had played baseball under his own name, whether out of honesty or stupidity, further fueled their outrage: Jim had never tried to be dishonest, yet he became a scapegoat for a system that was itself dishonest. In the years to come there would be many examples of countries that actually paid their athletes—against the rules—to play in

This bust of the Swedish king was Jim's trophy for winning the Olympic pentathlon. Not only was it taken back after he was stripped of his Olympic championships, but it disappeared. When one of his daughters, Grace, tried to reclaim the bust, along with the model of the Viking ship he had received from the czar of Russia for winning the decathlon, she was told they were "traveling" trophies that went to each new champion after each Olympics. But no one could tell her why no one else had ever gotten the trophies, or even where they were. Grace had hoped to place them in the Jim Thorpe Museum she was planning in Yale, Oklahoma.

the Olympics. But the millionaires and the aristocrats never cracked down on them.

Perhaps the main reason the AAU didn't deepen its investigation of professionalism was its fear that many others of America's most talented amateur athletes would also have been disqualified.

On the other hand, Jim did break the rules of his time. Maybe he was naive, but shouldn't he have gotten better advice from Pop Warner, who was pretty slick? Should Pop have been punished too? Even today, when sports rules are broken, the athletes usually are punished more severely than the coaches or administrators.

Jim was lucky to have close friends at Carlisle who reminded him that he had proven to the world he was the greatest athlete, with or without the medals. But they shared a deeper sorrow: To the Indians this was another story of broken treaties. They felt that no matter how shiny their buttons or perfect their diction or how many touchdowns they scored, Indians would never be treated fairly by whites.

It seemed to them that after Jim had bested the whites at every game they taught him, he was being punished for being too good.

Jim always tried to keep his pain private, but those closest to him saw it. Years later, while on the road with the New York Giants baseball team, John ("Chief") Meyers, a catcher who was also a Native American, awoke in the hotel room he shared with Jim to find him sitting in the dark, weeping.

"You know, Chief," Jim whispered, "I won those trophies. Fair and square."

9

Young and old loved him for what he was—a big, warm, fun-loving boy-man.

—CHARLOTTE THORPE

Pop Warner tried to make up for letting Jim take all the heat by helping him negotiate a rich baseball contract. Football was Jim's best sport, but those early pro football teams were small and unstable, nowhere near as popular as major college teams, while baseball was exploding into the national pastime. Several baseball teams made offers, figuring that Jim's fame would bring fans.

He joined the New York Giants. They offered a $6,000 annual salary plus a $5,000 signing bonus, an enormous amount in those days for an untested rookie. The day Jim signed the contract, he officially withdrew from Carlisle. He was going on twenty-six years old, ancient for a "student-athlete."

*Jim's wedding to Iva Miller was the Carlisle social event of 1913.
He stands behind his twenty-year-old bride, an honor student from
Oklahoma. It is thought she had little if any Indian ancestry, one of
the few whites to be educated in Indian schools.*

In October, after the baseball season, he
married Iva Miller in a ceremony at Carlisle
that kicked off days of dances, banquets and
parties. Their honeymoon was spent on a good-
will tour of Giant and Chicago White Sox players to Europe, Hawaii and Egypt. They
returned to an apartment in Manhattan near

the Giants' ballpark, the Polo Grounds.

John McGraw, the Giants' manager, was nearly as famous as Jim. Like Pop Warner, Mc-Graw was a tough, cocky celebrity coach, but unlike Pop, he didn't give players the room to develop their own styles and express their own personalities. He was a strict disciplinarian, and his traditional, textbook approach to baseball quickly clashed with Jim's freewheeling ways.

Pop may have been too loud and profane, often sleazy and even cowardly, but he always appreciated Jim as an athlete and a person. Mc-Graw was jealous of Jim's fame and mocked him for his unpolished skills. He made no real effort to make use of Jim's enormous natural gifts or his willingness and ability to learn quickly and work hard.

The relationship between McGraw and Jim became even more strained because of the manager's abuse. Once, after Jim missed a signal to steal, McGraw called him a "dumb Indian." Jim chased McGraw around the field until other Giants tackled and restrained him.

McGraw insulted Jim publicly, suggesting he was not smart enough for the complexities of

Jim's baseball skills were major league, but he was hired by the New York Giants more for his fame than his hitting. Because the manager was jealous of his stardom, Jim never got good coaching or the chance to play enough to improve.

the game and that he "couldn't hit the curve-
ball," an old baseball put-down. He accused Jim
of drinking too much and risking injury to other
players by challenging them to wrestling
matches. Actually, it was usually other Giants
who challenged Jim, eager to boast of pinning
the world's greatest athlete.

Jim spent most of his six seasons in the major
leagues (he also played for the Cincinnati Reds
and the Boston Braves) warming the bench. He
said he felt "like a sitting hen, not a ballplayer."

Jim was a favorite among his teammates because he was fun to be around, and because he
helped anyone in need. Later, Jim admitted that
his desire for a good time and his willingness to
share his wealth was the reason he was usually
broke.

Jim was also famous for his appetite.

"Boy, could that guy ever eat!" John Meyers
once exclaimed. "He'd order a beefsteak smoth-
ered in pork chops. And corned beef and cab-
bage, that was his favorite. He could down four
servings in one sitting!"

Teammates respected Jim as an athlete, and
some wondered how good he might have be-

come with patient coaching. By the time Jim left the game, baseball was buzzing over a new young phenom, Babe Ruth.

Jim played baseball for the money, but he got his real athletic kicks from football, which he played and coached into his forties. During the baseball off-season, he would volunteer as an assistant to Pop, at Carlisle and later at the University of Pittsburgh. Pop became more and more famous in his day, and he's still known because of the Pop Warner Leagues for young football beginners throughout America.

When the American Professional Football Association, which later became the National Football League, was created, Jim became player-coach-owner of the Canton (Ohio) Bulldogs. In 1920, he was elected president of the association. Pro football was a raucous game played by former All-Americas of varying ages. Fan loyalty and betting were fierce, the only similarity to today's high-tech game.

Jim was slower now but still a star. He never lost his kicking leg, and when it came to running and tackling, even an over-the-hill Jim could still dominate most players in their prime. Ernie

Jim's greatest athletic love was football, and he played into middle age. As a member of the Canton (Ohio) Bulldogs, he was an early player, owner and official of what would become the National Football League.

Nevers, a football star in his own right, was tackled by thirty-nine-year-old Jim and said he had never been hit so hard in his life. Jim's love for the game increased as he packed the Bulldogs with old Carlisle teammates. The postgame parties were pretty wild, too.

Later he formed an all-Indian football team called the Oorang Indians, named for its sponsor, a dog kennel. The players hammed it up with costumes and war dances as well as dog tricks and lasted two seasons before disbanding.

"Dad did not try to set himself up as an example for others to follow," wrote his daughter Charlotte in her book *Thorpe's Gold*, written with Brad Steiger. "Young and old loved him for what he was—a big, warm, fun-loving boy-man."

Jim returned to Oklahoma with Iva and their children and bought a house in a little town called Yale, where he would hunt and fish and see old friends. At times, though, he seemed closest to his dogs, according to Charlotte: "I think my father loved his coon dogs more than anything. He loved hunting and fishing the Indian way."

Jim was not the most responsible husband and father. His seven children always remembered him with affection, but few of them knew him very well. He had begun drinking even more heavily after his first son, James Jr., died in the 1918 influenza epidemic. Perhaps he was reminded of his brother Charlie's death. He would later say that Jim Jr.'s death was the worst time of his life, that the Olympic disappointment wasn't even in the same league. The stress of the tragedy probably was the main reason he and Iva divorced.

Newspaper stories about Jim Thorpe in later life portrayed him as a pathetic, broken spirit, as "Poor Jim," especially when he turned up broke or drunk or bar brawling or digging ditches. In 1932, when he couldn't afford a ticket to the Los Angeles Olympic Games, U.S. Vice-President Charles Curtis, who was part Indian, invited him to sit in his box. They watched Babe Didrikson, perhaps the greatest all-around female athlete in American history, and a lacrosse exhibition starring a young Mohawk who would be spotted by a Hollywood talent scout. Renamed Jay Silverheels, he was to play the Lone Ranger's sidekick, Tonto.

Jim sold the film rights to his life story for a mere $1,500. The movie that was made in 1953 starring Burt Lancaster, *Jim Thorpe—All-American*, was a box-office hit, but Jim didn't share in the profits.

His own children regarded him as a big kid—more an older brother or jolly uncle than a responsible, day-to-day father. He was happy around kids, and liked to romp and laugh and hand out candy.

Don't cry for Jim. He had his good times and he made his points and he left an important legacy. He went on to speak out against the abuses of the Bureau of Indian Affairs and the government control of Indians, and he lectured to thousands of schoolchildren about the richness and dignity of native life and culture.

His own children (three daughters with Iva—Gail, Charlotte and Grace; four sons—Carl Phillip, William, Richard and John—with his second wife, Freeda Kirkpatrick) remember him as a loving, caring man, sometimes more big brother than father, but a man who was proud of them and tried his best to make a living and give them a happy life.

In 1950, the Associated Press voted him the Male Athlete of the Half-Century. He was way ahead of runner-up Babe Ruth.

On March 28, 1953, in the Lomita, California, trailer in which he lived with his third wife, Patricia Askew, Jim Thorpe died of a heart attack. He was not quite sixty-six years old. It was the same year that Ike Eisenhower, the West Point football player who knocked himself out trying to tackle Jim, took office as President of the United States.

10

He is a great symbol to us.
—CHIEF OREN LYONS

"I met Jim Thorpe when I was growing up," said Chief Oren Lyons, Faithkeeper of the Onondaga Nation. "He knew my uncle, Ike Lyons, from Carlisle. He'd hang out here with his friends, and come watch our lacrosse games. I'd be trying to keep my eye on the ball, but I'd sneak glances at him. Powerful-looking man. Friendly. He is a great symbol to us."

For generations of Native Americans, the story of Jim Thorpe was both sad and inspiring. He was treated shabbily, they felt, cheated out of his medals and his prestige in the white world because he was an Indian; yet his accomplishments proved that an Indian could be the best in the world.

For Chief Lyons, a former All-America lacrosse goalie at Syracuse University, an artist and a world-renowned leader of the Haudenosaunee (Iroquois) Confederacy, the symbolism of Jim Thorpe was clear: The white world had to beat him down because he was so strong.

"Jim Thorpe showed up the white world," said Chief Lyons. "They were trying to prove we were savages, how else could they justify stealing our land and killing us? But here was Jim Thorpe and this raggedy group of savages from Carlisle, who just recently had their hair cut, just recently got shoes, and they're whipping West Point and Harvard. The white world took it as an insult. They had a respect for us in a way, but they had to beat us down."

Thirty years after his death, and mainly because of relentless pressure from his children, the International Olympic Committee reinstated Jim Thorpe. His name was returned to the rolls of the 1912 Olympic champions, and duplicate gold medals were struck and awarded to his children. (The IOC never gave back the bronze bust and the jewel-encrusted silver chalice, now said to be worth millions.)

It was a year after that, 1984, that forty male and female runners set out from the Onondaga Reservation near Syracuse, New York, to California, site of the Olympics, on a two-month, 3,600-mile journey called "The Great Jim Thorpe Longest Run."

So much had happened since Jim's death: The militant American Indian Movement had brought natives into the national struggle for civil rights; tribal colleges, teaching self-respect for natives' Indian identity, had sprung up; Indians had successfully used the legal system to win back land rights, fishing rights, mineral rights; Indian scholars were revealing the truth of their many Nations' histories. And white Americans were beginning to understand that Columbus' "discovery" of America was really an invasion, that the Indian reverence for nature was a starting point in saving the earth, even that there was something wrong in calling a team the "Redskins."

These were the messages the young people carried in the spring of 1984, messages worthy of a Runner for the Nation. They carried it through the late spring and early summer along

Two of the grandchildren of the great American Olympians Jim Thorpe and Jesse Owens carry the torch through New York City en route to the 1984 Games in Los Angeles. Bill Thorpe Jr. shares the honor with Gina Hemphill.

the northern rim of the United States, from the Onondaga Nation through the lands of the Oneida, the Winnebago, the Anishinabe, the Dakota, the Lakota, the Arapahoe, the Northern Cheyenne, the Ute, the Ouray, the Western Shoshone, to the lands of the California Indians and a four-day festival of art, dancing and lacrosse, the Jim Thorpe Memorial Powwow and Games. Two of Jim Thorpe's children, Gail and Grace, were there to meet the runners and thank them for keeping his spirit alive.

For the lacrosse players, the event had special significance; Jim Thorpe's story was also the story of their sport. In 1880, after more than a century of teaching Europeans how to play "bump hips," the Iroquois national team was charged with taking money in violation of amateur rules, even though they used the money to travel to overseas tournaments. Indians saw it as another white scheme to push them out of the way; they were winning too much. They were banned from international play for more than a hundred years, until the year of the Jim Thorpe Run, and then only because of a fierce campaign for reinstatement led by Chief Lyons.

Chief Oren Lyons (standing) of the Onondaga Nation, a leading Runner of the Haudenosaunee (Iroquois) Confederacy, remembers Thorpe as friendly and inspiring when Jim visited his reservation in the 1940s and '50s. Lyons went on to become one of the great college and club lacrosse players of his time, and a coach of the Iroquois national team. The player is Jimmy Bissell, Jr.

On the day before the runners set out, the old lacrosse star himself studied the determined faces of the young women and men as medicine men burned leaves at their feet and an elder chief reminded them to let nothing distract them from their mission.

Chief Lyons smiled and nodded and said: "Jim Thorpe was beaten, but he was never tamed. He was too strong an individual for that. He suffered, but he survived. And that is the story of our people."

FURTHER READING

Brown, Dee. *Bury My Heart at Wounded Knee*. New York: Holt, Rinehart & Winston, Inc., 1970.

Deloria, Vine, Jr. *Custer Died for Your Sins*. New York: Macmillan, 1969.

Levine, Peter. *American Sport: A Documentary History*. New Jersey: Prentice-Hall, Inc., 1989.

Lyons, Oren and John Mohawk, et al. *Exiled in the Land of the Free*. Santa Fe, NM: Clear Light Publishers, 1992.

Nabokov, Peter. *Indian Running*. Santa Barbara, CA: Capra Press, 1981.
———. *Native American Testimony*. New York: Penguin Books, 1991.

Newcombe, Jack. *The Best of the Athletic Boys*. New York: Doubleday, 1975.

Steiger, Brad and Charlotte Thorpe. *Thorpe's Gold*. New York: Dee/Quicksilver, 1984.

Wheeler, Robert W. *Pathway to Glory*. New York: Carlton Press, Inc., 1975.

INDEX